STORIES IN THE STARS

THE STORY OF PEGASUS

By Blanche Roesser

Gareth Stevens
PUBLISHING

[leveled reader]
science

Please visit our website, www.garethstevens.com. For a free color catalog of all our high-quality books, call toll free 1-800-542-2595 or fax 1-877-542-2596.

Library of Congress Cataloging-in-Publication Data

Roesser, Blanche, author.
The story of Pegasus / Blanche Roesser.
    pages cm. — (Stories in the stars)
Includes bibliographical references and index.
ISBN 978-1-4824-2677-9 (pbk.)
ISBN 978-1-4824-2678-6 (6 pack)
ISBN 978-1-4824-2679-3 (library binding)
1. Pegasus (Greek mythology)—Juvenile literature. 2. Mythology, Greek—Juvenile literature.
3. Constellations—Folklore—Juvenile literature. 4. Stars—Folklore—Juvenile literature. I. Title.
BL820.P4R64 2015
292.1'3—dc23
                                2015006059

Published in 2016 by
Gareth Stevens Publishing
111 East 14th Street, Suite 349
New York, NY 10003

Copyright © 2016 Gareth Stevens Publishing

Designer: Samantha DeMartin
Editor: Therese Shea

Photo credits: Cover, p. 1 Dorling Kindersley/Getty Images; p. 5 © iStockphoto.com/yganko; p. 7 DEA/A. DAGLI ORTI/De Agostini Picture Library/Getty Images; pp. 9, 15 Mondadori Portfolio/Mondadori Portfolio/Getty Images; p. 11 Piero di Cosimo/Wikimedia Commons; p. 13 © iStockphoto.com/SergeyMikhaylov; p. 17 Imagno/Hulton Fine Art Collection/Getty Images; p. 19 Jacqueline Abromeit/Shutterstock.com; p. 21 Sergii Tsololo/E+/Getty Images.

Printed in the United States of America

CPSIA compliance information: Batch #CS15GS: For further information contact Gareth Stevens, New York, New York at 1-800-542-2595.

CONTENTS

Boldface words appear in the glossary.

Meet Pegasus

A constellation is a group of stars that forms a shape. The Pegasus constellation is named for Pegasus, a horse with wings in Greek **myths**. Look at these stars connected by lines. Do you think the shape looks like a horse?

Perseus

Pegasus is in the story of Perseus, a Greek hero. Perseus lived on an island ruled by King Polydectes (pah-lee-DEHK-teez). The evil king wanted to marry Perseus's mother, but Perseus wouldn't let him. Polydectes planned to get rid of Perseus.

Polydectes asked Perseus to bring him the head of a monster named Medusa. Medusa was one of three Gorgons. These monsters had snakes for hair. Anyone who looked at them would turn to stone. Perseus agreed to kill Medusa.

The gods gave Perseus **sandals** with wings to help him fly and a sword to cut off Medusa's head. He got a **shield** to use as a **mirror** so he wouldn't have to look at her. He received a special helmet, too.

11

Perseus flew to the Gorgons' island. He used his shield to see them sleeping. When he put on the helmet, he became **invisible**! He used his sword to cut off Medusa's head. Some think the Perseus constellation shows this.

η
φ
γ
τ
θ
λ
ꙩ
α
ι
μ
ψ
δ
χ
β
ν
ξ
ω
π
ρ
ζ
ο

13

Bellerophon

Pegasus, the winged horse, came out of Medusa's neck and flew away. Later, a god gave a hero named Bellerophon (buh-LEHR-uh-fahn) a golden **bridle**. Bellerophon put the bridle on Pegasus to ride the horse.

15

Together, Bellerophon and Pegasus battled the Chimera (ky-MIHR-uh), a fire-breathing monster. They flew over the monster and killed it. One day, Bellerophon decided to fly Pegasus to Mount Olympus, the home of the gods.

Zeus (ZOOS), the king of the gods, became angry. He made Bellerophon fall to Earth. Pegasus kept flying. Zeus used the horse to carry his lightning and thunder. Then, Zeus placed Pegasus in the stars, where we can see him today.

19

The Great Square

The Pegasus constellation is one of the largest. We can see it from the end of summer through fall. Look for four bright stars that make up the "Great Square of Pegasus." Now find his legs. That's Pegasus the flying horse!

GLOSSARY

bridle: a set of straps that fits on a horse's head and is used for controlling it

invisible: unable to be seen

mirror: a piece of glass or shiny metal that shows images of things in front of it

myth: a story that was told by an ancient people to explain something

sandal: a light, open shoe with straps worn during warm weather

shield: a large piece of metal, wood, or other matter carried for protection

FOR MORE INFORMATION

BOOKS

Beaumont, Steve. *Drawing Pegasus and Other Winged Wonders.* London, England: Franklin Watts, 2011.

Davidson, Susanna. *The Story of Pegasus.* London, England: Usborne Publishing, 2011.

Namm, Diane. *Roman Myths: Retold from the Classic Originals.* New York, NY: Sterling Publishing, 2014.

WEBSITES

Great Square of Pegasus: Easy to See
earthsky.org/favorite-star-patterns/great-square-of-pegasus-wings-in-sept-equinox
Learn how to find Pegasus in the night sky.

Pegasus
greece.mrdonn.org/greekgods/pegasus.html
Read more about Pegasus and find links to other myths.

INDEX

MATH LAB
FOR KIDS

Tangrams and Puzzles

Fun, Hands-on Activities
for Learning Math

REBECCA RAPOPORT AND J.A. YODER

QUARRY

Brimming with creative inspiration, how-to projects, and useful information to enrich your everyday life, Quarto Knows is a favorite destination for those pursuing their interests and passions. Visit our site and dig deeper with our books into your area of interest: Quarto Creates, Quarto Cooks, Quarto Homes, Quarto Lives, Quarto Drives, Quarto Explores, Quarto Gifts, or Quarto Kids.

First Published in 2017 by Quarry Books, an imprint of The Quarto Group,
100 Cummings Center, Suite 265-D, Beverly, MA 01915, USA.
T (978) 282-9590 F (978) 283-2742 QuartoKnows.com

Quarry Books titles are also available at discount for retail, wholesale, promotional, and bulk purchase. For details, contact the Special Sales Manager by email at specialsales@quarto.com or by mail at The Quarto Group, Attn: Special Sales Manager, 401 Second Avenue North, Suite 310, Minneapolis, MN 55401, USA.

10 9 8 7 6 5 4 3 2 1

ISBN: 978-1-63159-447-2

Content for this book was originally found in Math Lab for Kids by Rebecca Rapoport and J.A. Yoder (Quarry Books, 2017)

Design: Laura Shaw Design, Inc
Page Layout: Alex Youngblood
Photography: Glenn Scott Photography
Illustration: J.A. Yoder & Rebecca Rapoport

Printed in USA

PUBLISHER'S NOTE Quarry Books would like to thank the staff and students at Birches School in Lincoln, Massachusetts, which graciously agreed to host the kid's photography for this book. We are especially grateful to Cecily Wardell, Director of Admissions and Placement, who generously gave our authors, art director, and photographer access to their facilities and helped us coordinate their students' participation to minimize disruption.

CONTENTS

INTRODUCTION

This is your introduction to the gorgeous, exciting, beautiful math that only professionals see. What's truly astounding is that it's *accessible,* even to six- to ten-year-olds. We think that if more kids had a chance to play with real math, there would be far more mathematicians in the world.

Most people think you learn math by climbing a sort of ladder: first addition, then subtraction, then multiplication, then fractions, and so on. In fact, math is much more like a tree. There are many different areas of math, most of which are never seen in school. Plenty of this lovely and woefully ignored math doesn't require any previous knowledge. It's accessible to everyone, if they just knew it existed.

People who read this book sometimes ask us, "How is this math?" Kids cut and tape and sew and color. They imagine walking over bridges, reproducing the same problem that spawned an entire field of mathematics. They draw enormous shapes in parking lots. It may not look like math since there are whole chapters with no pencils or memorization or calculators—but we assure you, the math you're about to encounter is much closer to what actual mathematicians do.

Mathematicians play. They come up with interesting questions and investigate possible solutions. This often results in a lot of dead ends, but mathematicians know that failure provides a great chance to learn. In this book, you'll have a chance to think like a mathematician and experiment with a given idea to see what you can discover. That approach of just fiddling around with a problem and seeing what falls out is an extremely common and useful technique that mathematicians employ. If you take nothing else away from this book, learning to just try something—anything—and seeing what develops is a great skill for math, science, engineering, writing, and, well, life!

This is your opportunity, your gateway, into little-known worlds of math. Turn the page and explore for yourself.

HOW TO USE THIS BOOK

All of the material in this book has been successfully play-tested by six- to ten-year-olds. We do assume elementary students will have a guide (parent/teacher/older sibling) to help them work through the labs. Much of the material should be interesting to middle school, high school, and adult students. There are cases where older kids will be able to try a more advanced technique and younger kids will do something easier, or may need a little help. Younger kids may need assistance with certain labs (tying knots, threading needles, cutting with scissors, etc.).

Each section in this book contains an introductory Think About It question. The question is always related to the section's content and is meant to be played with before moving on to the labs. This gives you the opportunity to experiment with the topic before we've introduced any formal concepts. Sometimes we come back to the Think About It problem within the chapter and answer it directly. Sometimes we don't. (In that case, if you're curious, check the Hints and Solutions section.) In general, we hope students will have time to experiment and not just race through each lab. Real math is so much more about curiosity and experimentation than most people realize.

Each topic scratches the surface of a whole field of mathematics. If you're interested in more on any given topic, we've included some good sources in the Resources page.

TERRIFIC TANGRAMS

Tangrams were invented in China hundreds of years ago. Legend has it that a Chinese emperor's servant dropped a precious tile that broke into seven pieces. As the servant attempted to reassemble the tile, he discovered he could create many beautiful shapes from the seven pieces.

Tangram puzzles are a bit like jigsaw puzzles, except you always use the same seven pieces to create different shapes. In addition to being fun, solving tangram puzzles builds problem-solving skills, develops geometric intuition, and improves pattern recognition and design abilities.

Think About It

How can the same seven pieces make a square and also a square that is missing some space inside (like the pictures below)?

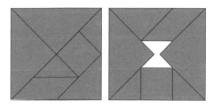

TANGRAM BASICS

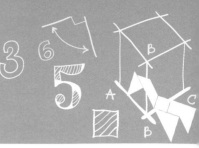

Materials

✔ Set of tangrams

Note: *There is a set of tangrams on page 14 that you can copy and cut up. If you want a more durable set, they're easy to buy online.*

RULES FOR TANGRAMS

1. Use all seven tangram pieces (also called *tans*) for every puzzle.

2. Try different arrangements of the pieces to exactly match the picture.

3. You may have to flip the pieces over to solve the puzzles.

4. If you are having trouble, print out a full-size version of the puzzle from our website so the tangram pieces will fit inside. This will make the puzzles easier to solve.

Tangram puzzles always use the same seven pieces to make a picture.

STARTER TANGRAMS

See solutions on page 15.

1. Can you make a bat with your seven tangrams **(fig. 1)**?

2. Can you make a giraffe with your seven tangrams **(fig. 2)**?

3. Can you make a helicopter with your seven tangrams **(fig. 3)**?

4. Can you make a turtle with your seven tangrams **(fig. 4)**?

5. Can you make a rabbit with your seven tangrams **(fig. 5)**?

FIG. 1

FIG. 2

FIG. 3

FIG. 4

FIG. 5

7

Materials

✔ Set of tangrams (*see page 14*)

You can print out full-size versions of these puzzles from our website.

What else can you make with your set of tangrams?

NEXT-LEVEL TANGRAMS

See solutions on page 15.

1. Can you make a cat with your seven tangrams **(fig. 1)**?

2. Can you make a dog with your seven tangrams **(fig. 2)**?

3. Can you make a candle with your seven tangrams **(fig. 3)**?

4. Can you make a rocket with your seven tangrams **(fig. 4)**?

5. Can you make a square with your seven tangrams **(fig. 5)**?

FIG. 1

FIG. 2

FIG. 3

FIG. 4

FIG. 5

Tangrams Party

Making your own tangram puzzle is easier than you think. Here are two methods.

METHOD 1

1. Move your tangrams around until you find a shape you like.

2. Trace the outline.

3. Name your tangram.

4. Challenge your friend(s) to solve it!

METHOD 2

1. Think of a shape you would like to make and see if you and your friend(s) can make it. For example, can you make all 26 letters of the alphabet or the numbers 0 through 9 with your tangrams? What about a triangle?

2. Once you have a solution you like, trace the outline.

3. Trade puzzles with your friend(s) and solve each other's tangrams.

Materials

✔ Set of tangrams (see page 14)

✔ Pencil

✔ Paper

✔ At least two people

Materials

✔ 2 sets of tangrams (*see page 14*)

Let's take tangrams to a whole new level! If you get stuck, print out the full-size versions from our website.

TANGRAMS CHALLENGE

1. Can you make a house with your seven tangrams **(fig. 1)**?

2. Can you make a boat with your seven tangrams **(fig. 2)**?

3. Can you make an arrow with your seven tangrams **(fig. 3)**?

4. Can you make a double arrow with your seven tangrams **(fig. 4)**?

5. Can you make these two bridges **(fig. 5)**? (You'll need a set of tangrams for each bridge.)

6. Can you make these monks using your seven tangrams **(fig. 6)**? This puzzle was created by English mathematician Henry Ernest Dudeny (1857–1930). Two monks look the same, but one is missing a foot. (You'll need a full set of seven tangrams for each monk.)

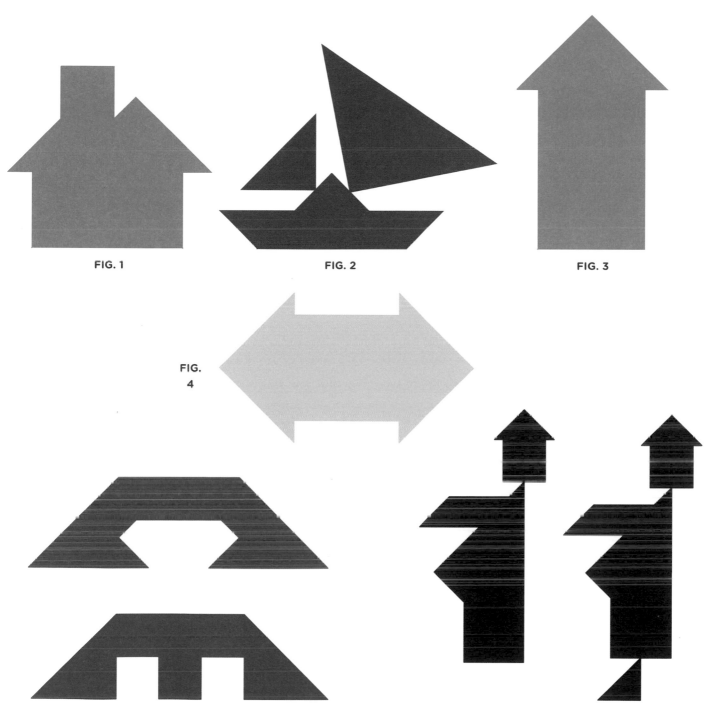

FIG. 1

FIG. 2

FIG. 3

FIG. 4

FIG. 5

FIG. 6

COPY: TANGRAMS

See Labs 1-3, pages 5-13.

HINTS AND SOLUTIONS

I. TERRIFIC TANGRAMS

Think About It:

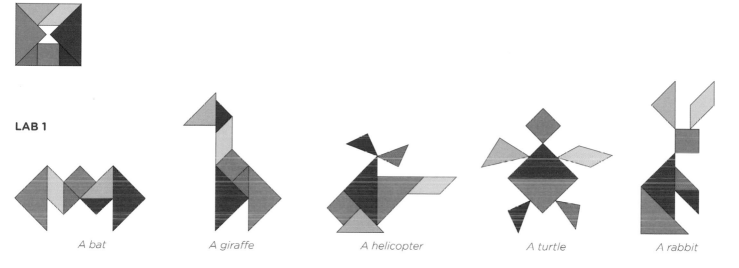

LAB 1

A bat

A giraffe

A helicopter

A turtle

A rabbit

LAB 2

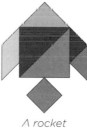

A cat

A dog

A candle

A rocket

A square

HINTS AND SOLUTIONS continued

LAB 3

A house

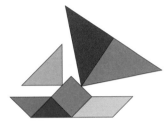

A boat

An arrow

A double arrow

Two bridges

Two monks

TOOTHPICK PUZZLES

Toothpick puzzles (sometimes called matchstick puzzles) ask you to rearrange a given pattern of sticks into a second pattern according to a set of rules. They range from easy to very difficult, and are great brainteasers to encourage mathematical thinking—playing with ideas and seeing what comes out.

In addition to being fun, these puzzles build skills in rule-following, recognizing shapes, and counting. Because they are well suited to trial-and-error techniques, they can be a great tool to build problem-solving confidence, because you can just keep trying different solutions until you find one that works. The willingness to keep trying things when you don't know the answer is one of the most important mathematical skills there is.

Think About It

How many triangles can you find in this image?
(*Hint*: The answer is greater than six!)

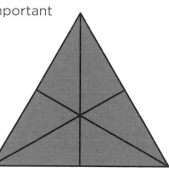

Materials

✔ Toothpicks, matchsticks, or craft sticks

Learn to solve toothpick puzzles. Start with your toothpicks as shown in the figures. Then follow the instructions to transform the shapes.

ACTIVITY 1: PRACTICE PUZZLE

Hint: If a puzzle doesn't say that the squares or triangles need to be exactly the same size, they can be different sizes!

1. Remove two sticks from the puzzle in **fig. 1** to leave two squares.

2. The resulting shape has exactly two squares **(fig. 2)**—but they overlap **(fig. 3)**!

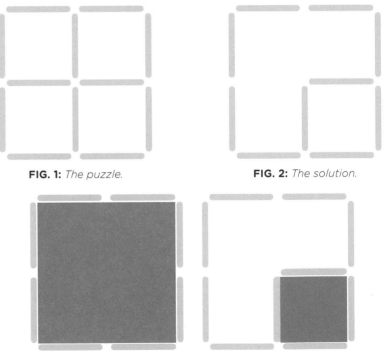

FIG. 1: *The puzzle.*

FIG. 2: *The solution.*

FIG. 3: *Two overlapping squares.*

ACTIVITY 2: STARTER PUZZLES

For solutions, see page 24.

1. Move two sticks to create two equal-size triangles **(fig. 4)**.

2. Move two sticks to make two equal-size squares **(fig. 5)**.

3. Start with five triangles. (Can you find them all?) Remove two sticks to leave exactly two triangles **(fig. 6)**.

4. Move three sticks to create five squares **(fig. 7)**.

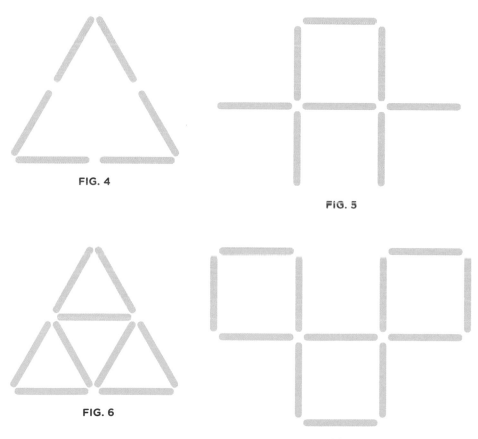

FIG. 4

FIG. 5

FIG. 6

FIG. 7

MATH TECHNIQUE
Trial and Error

This technique helps you solve a puzzle when you don't even know where to start! When you aren't sure how to begin solving a problem, use *trial and error.*

This problem-solving method involves trying something—anything—even if you don't think it will work, and then looking carefully at the result to see what happened. If it isn't what you wanted, go back to the beginning, and try something different. Keep trying things (and keep carefully looking at the result!) until you either find the solution or begin to get an idea of how the problem works, which may lead to a more efficient way to solve it.

For example, if a toothpick puzzle says "remove two sticks" to produce a particular result, start by just picking up any two sticks from the puzzle. What shapes are you left with? Could this be the solution to the puzzle? If not, put the sticks back, and try picking up two different sticks. Keep trying until you succeed!

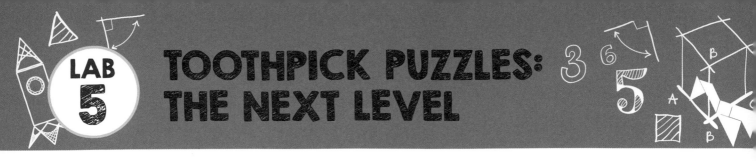
Materials

✔ Toothpicks, matchsticks, or craft sticks

✔ Bead or penny, for fish puzzle

These puzzles are a little trickier! Start with your toothpicks as shown in the figures. Then follow the instructions to transform the shapes.

TRY MORE COMPLEX PUZZLES

See pages 24–25 for solutions.

1. Start with two small diamonds. Move four sticks to end up with one large diamond **(fig. 1)**.

2. Can you transform the spiral of sticks into two squares by moving three sticks **(fig. 2)**?

3. Remove three sticks to end up with four equal-size squares. Can you also figure out how to remove four sticks and end up with four equal-size squares **(fig. 3)**?

4. Move two sticks to end up with four equal-size squares **(fig. 4)**.

5. Start with a fish swimming to the right. Without moving the eye, can you move two sticks so that the fish is swimming straight up **(fig. 5)**?

6. Remove four sticks to end up with four equal-size triangles **(fig. 6)**.

FIG. 1

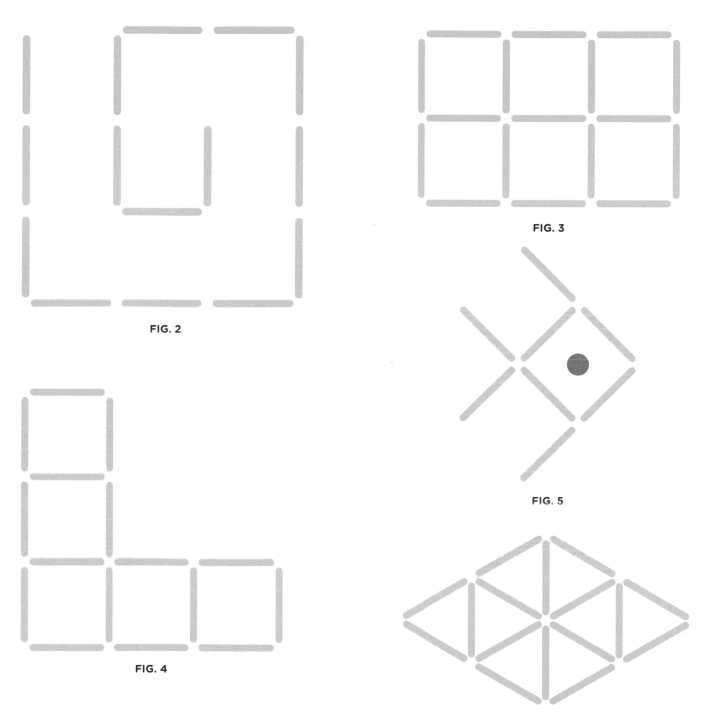

FIG. 2

FIG. 3

FIG. 4

FIG. 5

FIG. 6

Materials

✔ Toothpicks, matchsticks, or craft sticks

✔ Pebble, bead, or penny for cup puzzle

MATH MEET
Invent Your Own Toothpick Puzzle

Stump your friends and family!

1. Make an arrangement of toothpicks.

2. Remov, add, or move toothpicks to make a second shape.

3. If you aren't happy with the possible puzzles from your starting arrangement, go back to step 1 and try again!

Puzzle makers try lots of configurations to invent puzzles. When you've found an arrangement you like, draw the starting placement for the sticks and write the instructions for the puzzle. On a separate paper, you might want to draw out the answer. Now you can share your puzzle with everyone!

Even more mind-bending puzzles! Start with your toothpicks as shown in the figures. Then follow the instructions to transform the shapes.

PUZZLE PALOOZA

See page 25 for solutions.

1. This is two puzzles in one **(fig. 1)**.

- Move four sticks to get three equal squares.

- Move two sticks to make two rectangles.

2. Start with five squares **(fig. 2)**. Move two sticks so there are no squares left, but instead four identical shapes.

3. Move four sticks to create two arrows, each half the size of the starting arrow **(fig. 3)**.

4. Start with a ball inside a cup **(fig. 4)**. Move two sticks so that the ball is outside the cup. The cup should be the same size and shape—and don't move the ball!

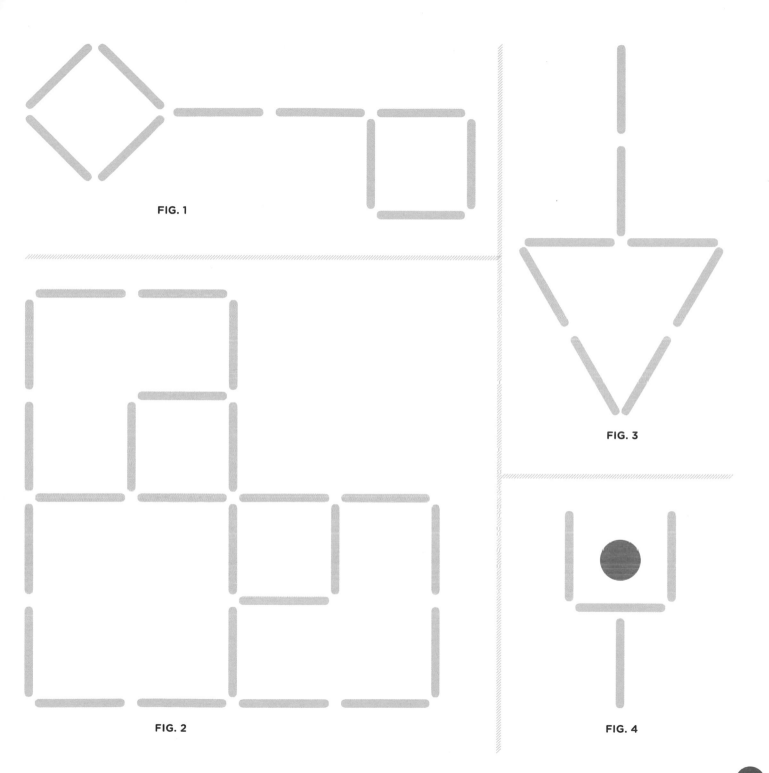

FIG. 1

FIG. 2

FIG. 3

FIG. 4

HINTS AND SOLUTIONS

2. TOOTHPICK PUZZLES

Think About It: There are 16 triangles in the image.

LAB 4, Activity 2:

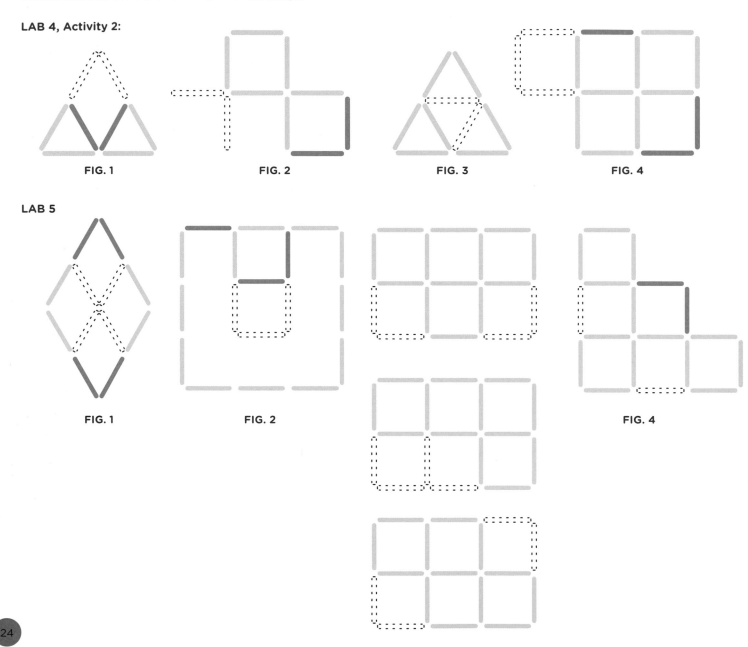

FIG. 1   FIG. 2   FIG. 3   FIG. 4

LAB 5

FIG. 1   FIG. 2   FIG. 4

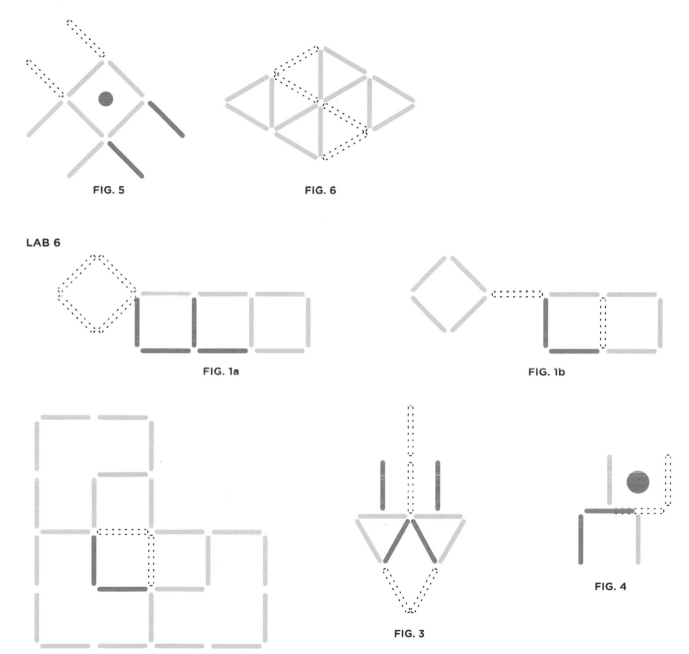

FIG. 5

FIG. 6

LAB 6

FIG. 1a

FIG. 1b

FIG. 2

FIG. 3

FIG. 4

Materials

✔ Printouts of the following maps from our website: **Checkerboard Map, Modified Checkerboard Map** (*see page 30*), **Triangle Map 1, Triangle Map 2,**

✔ Crayons, markers, or colored pencils (at least four colors)

✔ Four different colors of beads, counters, or other items that won't roll once placed on a piece of paper, or four colors of modeling clay

Welcome to the world of map coloring! In this lab, learn to use the fewest colors possible to fill in various maps.

HOW MANY COLORS?

1. Color the *Checkerboard Map* with as few colors as possible, making sure to use different colors for shapes that are next to each other. How many colors do you need **(fig. 1)**? You could use as many as nine colors but you only need two **(fig. 2)**. Actually, some kids might even use more than one color for a single square. That's pretty, but for this chapter, let's limit each region to a single color.

2. How many colors do you need for the *Modified Checkerboard Map*? Try it and see **(fig. 3)**.

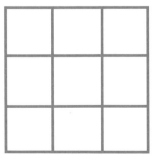

FIG. 1: *Color the checkerboard with as few colors as possible.*

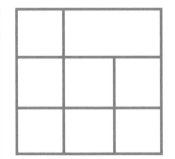

FIG. 2: *You only need two colors.*

FIG. 3: *Color the modified checkerboard.*

Now that you've colored some maps, you'll see that our initial rule to use "as few colors as possible" wasn't precise enough. For the rest of this chapter, we'll use the following *map coloring rules*:

- Each region should get exactly one color.

- Use as few colors as possible.

- When two areas touch along a side, they need to be different colors.

- If areas only touch on a corner, it's okay for them to be the same color.

3. Try coloring *Triangle Map 1* **(fig. 4)** and *Triangle Map 2* **(fig. 5)**. The first one only needs two colors. The second one needs three.

Questions

- What were your strategies for figuring out which colors to use in order to have the fewest number possible?

- Were there frequently used patterns in your colorings?

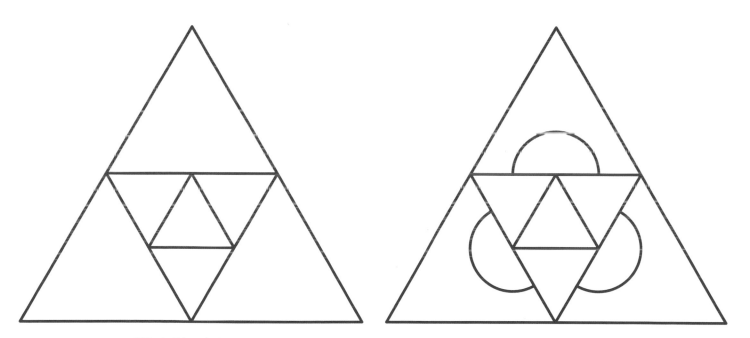

FIG. 4: *Triangle Map 1.*　　　　**FIG. 5:** *Triangle Map 2.*

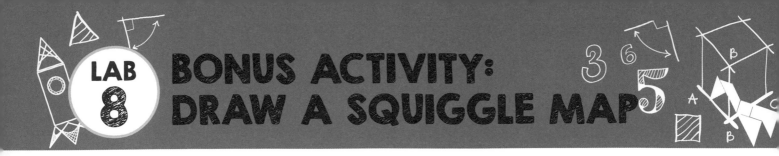

BONUS ACTIVITY: DRAW A SQUIGGLE MAP

Materials

✔ Pencil

✔ Several blank sheets of paper

✔ Crayons, markers, or colored pencils

Any picture you draw with a pencil or pen can be thought of as a map. Learn to draw and color a map made from a single squiggly line.

DRAW A SQUIGGLE MAP

1. Put your pencil on a clean sheet of paper.

2. Draw a long, curving line that goes anywhere on the paper **(fig. 1)**. Do not take the pencil off the paper or go off an edge. (The big red dot shows where you started your squiggle. You don't need to draw a big dot on your picture.)

3. The line you are drawing can cross itself any number of times anywhere on the paper **(fig. 2)**.

4. Your map is finished when your pencil gets back to the starting point. You'll end up with a tangled squiggle **(fig. 3)**.

5. Using the techniques you learned in the previous labs, fill in your squiggle map with as few colors as possible **(fig. 4)**.

6. Try making and coloring more squiggle maps on your own.

TRY THIS!

Every squiggle map can be fully colored with just two colors. Can you figure out why?

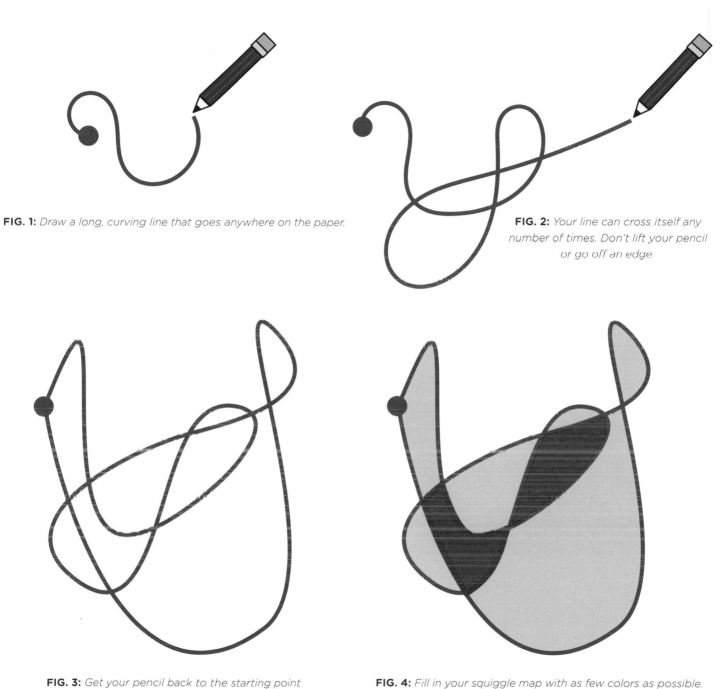

FIG. 1: *Draw a long, curving line that goes anywhere on the paper.*

FIG. 2: *Your line can cross itself any number of times. Don't lift your pencil or go off an edge.*

FIG. 3: *Get your pencil back to the starting point*

FIG. 4: *Fill in your squiggle map with as few colors as possible.*

COPY: MODIFIED CHECKERBOARD MAP

See Lab 7, pages 26-27.

HINTS AND SOLUTIONS

BONUS ACTIVITY: MAP COLORING BASICS

LAB 7

Step 2: There are multiple possible solutions, but you shouldn't need more than three colors.

Step 3: There are multiple possible solutions, but you shouldn't need more than two colors for Triangle Map 1 and three colors for Triangle Map 2.

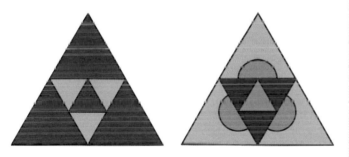

RESOURCES

Go to **mathlabforkids.com** or **quartoknows.com/page/math-lab** for printable versions of some exercises and pull-out pages in this book.

National Council of Teachers of Mathematics
There is some great material in the "Classroom Resources" section. www.nctm.org

Fractal Foundation
Check out the Fractivities and other content in the Explore Fractals section. http://fractalfoundation.org

Zome
Geometric building toy. http://zometool.com

ACKNOWLEDGMENTS

Rebecca would like to thank her parents, Ron and Joan, for teaching her to write clearly, concisely, and grammatically correctly. And a second round of thanks to her father for making her think writing a book is a normal thing to do.

She would also like to thank her husband, Dean, for his support throughout the process.

Rebecca's fabulous eldest child, Allanna, caused her to realize this book needed to be written. Allanna and her brother, the forever inquisitive Zack, were not only enthusiastic about the idea of Mom writing a book but also cheerfully play-tested some of the book's content. Rebecca looks forward to working through all the labs with her youngest, Xander, when he's old enough. In the meantime, she appreciates the good humor and joy all three bring into her life every day.

We would both like to acknowledge how much fun it was to work on this book together. It was a great collaborative effort and resulted in something we're both proud of. The book also gave us a wonderful opportunity to continue the meaningful work we began at the STEAM (science, technology, engineering, art, and math) after-school enrichment center we helped build.

J.A. would like to thank Rebecca for her patience, her enthusiasm, and for the opportunity for this collaboration that taught each of us some new things and strengthened our long-time friendship. This was a wonderful chance to improve my own ideas by bouncing them off someone I trust, learn a bunch of really cool new stuff (whether it made it into the book or not!), and share many truly terrible math jokes.

We owe a big debt of gratitude to all the people who helped us test and hone the book's content, especially the staff and students of Birches School in Lincoln, Massachusetts, whose cheerful faces brighten up this book's pages.

J.A.'s math professor mother, Kathie, provided valuable feedback on the book's content and her enthusiasm in working every lab made us happy.

Of course, we'd like to thank our editor, Joy, and Tiffany for pitching the book idea to us and Quarry in the first place. Meredith and Anne were invaluable in making this book look as good as it does.

Finally, we'd like to thank all the staff at Quarry Books who worked on this book for helping us put such a beautiful, full-color romp through math out into the world.

ABOUT THE AUTHORS

Rebecca Rapoport holds degrees in mathematics from Harvard and Michigan State. From her first job out of college, as one of the pioneers of Harvard's Internet education offerings, she has been passionate about encouraging her love of math in others.

As an early contributor to both retail giant Amazon.com and Akamai Technologies, the No. 1 firm in cloud computing, Rapoport played a key role in several elements of the Internet revolution.

Rapoport returned to her first love, education, as an innovator of new methods to introduce children and adults to the critically important world of STEM as COO of Einstein's Workshop, an enrichment center dedicated to helping kids explore the creative side of science, technology, engineering, art, and math. One of their classes for six- to ten-year-olds is Recreational Math, which inspired the creation of this book.

Currently, Rapoport is developing and teaching innovative math curricula at Boston-area schools.

J.A. Yoder holds a degree in computer science from Caltech. She is an educator and engineer who has a lifetime love of puzzles and patterns. Her educational philosophy is that hands-on creative work is both the most fun and the most effective way to learn. She developed and taught the original hands-on-math lessons for an after-school program that eventually inspired this book. Some of her happiest memories come from "eureka moments"—either from learning something that makes a dozen other things suddenly make sense, or the sense of accomplishment that comes from solving a clever puzzle. The only thing better is sharing this joy with others.